Haikus
of
Soul

AUTLEY I. SALAHUDDIN

OMNIWORKS

Haikus of Soul by Autley I. Salahuddin

Published by OmniWorks International
2950 Northwest 99 Street
Miami, FL 33147
www.omniworksintl.com

Cover design by OmniWorks International

"Sunset Lavender Field" cover image by "Stockcake.com" and used with permission.
"Panama" image by "ClipartBuff" via www.etsy.com and used with permission.
"Pole Dancer" image the property of Autley I. Salahuddin
"Love's Pimp" image by "Partydudes.co", New Zealand and used with permission.

Paperback ISBN: 979-8-9994981-4-4
Hardback ISBN: 979-8-9994981-8-2
E-Book ISBN: 979-8-9994981-9-9

10 9 8 7 6 5 4 3 2 1
Printed in the United States of America

DEDICATION

To the woman I once loved and experimented with sexually, who sparked the journey of this book. When her post-graduate studies tasked her with writing haikus, a form unknown to both of us, she quickly educated herself and me, and then challenged me to write my own. This collection of haikus, born from that inspiration, reflects my time in incarceration, grappling with love, lust, and confusion. I dedicate this book to her - my "starting p▲int."

ACKNOWLEDGMENTS

Indeed, all praise is due to Allah, the only deity in truth deserving of any and all forms of worship, Possessor of the most beautiful names and qualities ever imagined, realized, considered, comprehended, or understood. Abundant peace and blessings are extended to the Prophet Muhammad; may Allah raise him to the loftiest of ranks and grant him peace, an exemplary human whose character, level of acceptance, and tolerance I strive to emulate daily in my life.

Beyond this fundamental truth, a special thank you to Oni, who first exposed me to the bottomless depths of inner expression and the artistry of spoken word. Her confidence and comfort in sharing that part of herself was the catalyst that inspired me to discover my own expression, laying the foundation for all my creative sharing, including these haikus.

CONTENTS

PERSPECTIVE

Haikus of Soul: Love, Lust & Confusion is a quiet, reflective journey told through the lens of haiku. I'll admit, haiku wasn't a style I was familiar with before reading this book, but I'm grateful for the opportunity to explore it through my friend's eyes.

Each poem offers a glimpse into memory, longing, and connection. Whether he's honoring a legendary voice like Teena Marie in 'Lady of Soul', or capturing the simple complexities of love, the author uses small, vivid details to tell larger emotional stories.

This body of work feels personal—like reading someone's diary in poetic form. The poems aren't flashy or overly complex. Instead, they serve as quiet reminders of love, nostalgia, and the simple moments that make us human.

It may not be a fast-paced or traditional book of poetry—but that's the beauty of it. It encourages stillness, reflection, and the courage to express what's often hard to say out loud.

–Delina Hill-Brooker

INTRODUCTION

It's a rainy August morning that marks day nine of my 17th year of incarceration. I pen these words to you from behind this wall, knowing what I want to convey, yet the task is more complex than it seems. While those who knew me prior to this experience might describe me as outgoing and with words that speak to achievement, scholarship, and drive, those who live and have lived with me behind this wall will probably describe me as being reserved, quiet, observant, and disciplined. I am, in truth, the sum total of both observations. I am a man who has grown to be comfortable within my own skin and to prefer my own company. The people-pleaser I once was is gone; I prefer to move solo and could care less if you like me.

I am Autley Ibn-Faheem Salahuddin, an American Muslim born and raised in Miami, Florida. I believe the moniker "American Muslim" is fitting because I am a Muslim raised within the vast influences and pressures of American culture. Considering the complexity of this

HAIKUS OF SOUL

paradox is challenging not only in thought but also in the daily reality of living it. America is a country where laws are often changed to accommodate the ever-shifting desires of its people, whereas the orthodox practice of Islam, according to its pious predecessors, is fixed and unchanging. Although often perceived as too rigid, Islam is a way of life, contrary to mainstream belief, that is perfectly fitting for any period of time.

Most don't know and find it difficult to believe that I grew up with low self-esteem, which I believe was overshadowed because I excelled academically. It seems that my mental health, which wasn't as researched and understood then as it is now, wasn't a factor for a young black man so long as he was on the road to achieving academically according to the norms and expectations of American society.

There is, however, a lingering danger in judging a book by its cover. I can remember publicly voicing at a high school seminar that I had considered committing suicide. The subsequent investigation of that confession was seen as causing such distress, which resulted in the issue being dismissed and the blame for the suicidal thoughts being placed on me. It's amazing to consider how that experience came full circle, as my incarceration stems from my inability to cope with a mental health condition I had carried in society for too long.

This inability was the culmination of a professional betrayal where, as a self-employed electrical contractor, my contract with a major corporation was breached and thousands of dollars were stolen, leading to my termination as a whistleblower. The resulting financial ruin triggered a cascade of legal and debt-collection battles that pushed me to my breaking point. My anger, which had started as an emotional and psychological burden, erupted physically when I shot my neighbor without cause. This led to my arrest, and it was while I was in custody that a court-ordered psychological evaluation diagnosed my condition as an 'Adjustment Disorder Unspecified,' a condition caused by the stress endured prior to my breakdown.

The court-ordered evaluation, which should have served as my defense, was deliberately suppressed by the trial judge and every appellate court thereafter, up to the United States Supreme Court. As a result, the court's action prevented the victim from ever knowing the reason for what happened, and it denied me any form of legal remedy or relief. My legal journey, and everything that led to it, became a tragic demonstration of how unsupported mental health is a destroyer of lives.

Please understand that my mental health struggles did not commence once I became an entrepreneur; the signs have been present and identified for all of my life, but I was made to function with them. In my home, there was a saying: "It's not what you say, but how you say it." But the reality was, if you said it, whatever it was, in a manner that was perceived as "wrong," there were painful consequences of various kinds—mentally, emotionally, and occasionally physically.

There were always two ever-present challenges to communicating. The first was convincing myself that it was okay to *attempt* to say something. The second was the fear that what I said could be misconstrued as disrespect, which was never my intention.

The mental and emotional strain of constantly considering these challenges was exhausting and suffocating, as I needed to express what was on my heart. Finally, I found a refuge in the comfort of written expression. I just had to get it out; otherwise, I would explode.

No one could censor my pen, and they didn't have the right to. My heart desperately needed to breathe; it was suffocating from its own silence, as the conditions for speaking were too ambiguous to ever be met. Throughout my life, when the written expressions of my heart reached the eyes and were conveyed to the heart, they brought tears to the eyes of many who didn't even care to consider how their own self-absorption affected someone like me.

The consequence of being afraid to express your truth in a comfortable environment, like home, is that your confidence and ability to express yourself are non-existent and paralyzed in any environment of discomfort. You grow to dread any semblance of confrontation because your living experiences prove that confrontation could and often does lead to pain, in some form. So you change who you are in countless ways to cater to people who, perhaps even subconsciously, seem to only truly care about themselves, their ego's desires, and self-interests. You condition yourself to accept never receiving the benefit of the doubt. It is foreign having someone to care or inquire about how you feel and what is important to you. You are alive but not living, as you have a voice but are silenced from fear and suffocating within as a result.

When I write, my heart breathes, but more importantly, it exhales. The inhalation is what it receives from people, both with and without intent, while the exhalation is the *release* of all that I have felt from it. Writing is my safe space. It is the medium where I have the difficult conversations within that I was too afraid to have in person because of perceived and real consequences, free from bias, judgment, and assumptions. It is where the voice of my heart's truth is most authentic and can be expressed without fear.

This introduction is a gateway to my heart's voice, and this debut book serves as a formal introduction to my written expression and its vital role in my survival and existence. These haikus are not simply poems, but an "exhalation"–each one a captured breath, a small moment of release for my heart, both priceless and timeless. Until our hearts meet again within the confines of some text, this connection will remain to be continued.

–Autley I. Salahuddin

WHAT IS A HAIKU?

A haiku is a brief, three-line poetic form that traditionally captures fleeting moments.

The *first* line can only contain *five* syllables.
The *second* line only *seven* syllables, and...
The *third* line only *five* syllables.

In this collection, "*Haikus of Soul*," each poem is a raw, unfiltered expression of my spirit and experiences while incarcerated. Here is an example of a haiku from these pages:

SALAHUDDIN
---------- (a Haiku) ----------
Four-syllable name,
Unmistakenly unique,
Unforgettable.

Enjoy.

PART ONE

Love

GREAT EXPECTATIONS
---------- (a Haiku) ----------
Frosted flakes - big bowl,
Ice cold vanilla Soy milk,
Can't wait to leave here.

LOVE'S HUT
---------- (a Haiku) ----------
Consider this truth,
Pizza Hut pizza and wings,
Are my favorite.

A pan or stuffed crust,
Chicken supreme or just cheese,
Life's simple pleasures.

LOVE'S CRAVE
---------- (a Haiku) ----------
Can't forget about,
Popeye's famous fried chicken,
I think I'm hungry.

LADY OF SOUL
---------- (a Haiku) ----------
Ms. Teena Marie,
A taste of white chocolate,
How I miss your voice.

LOVE'S MEMORY
---------- (a Haiku) ----------
Just thinking of you,
Random thoughts of yesterday,
Seem so far away.

MATRIMONY
---------- (a Haiku) ----------
I want to embrace,
Life's simple pleasures with you,
Until my last breath.

MY JOY
---------- (a Haiku) ----------
Fixin' you breakfast,
In bed - toast, grits and cheese eggs,
With apple butter.

ELEMENTAL LOVE
---------- (a Haiku) ----------
Can reality...,
Lack the element of "love"?
That's impossible!

LOVE'S SEARCH
---------- (a Haiku) ----------
I'm searching my heart,
Sometimes I feel out of touch,
With reality.

LOVE'S REFLECTION
---------- (a Haiku) ----------
It's clear I'm searching,
My heart's depths for direction,
To my reflection.

GENUINE LOVE
---------- (a Haiku) ----------
"Love" knows no color,
Cares not for gender or race,
Only a pure place.

LOVE'S ABODE
---------- (a Haiku) ----------
I offer my heart,
For "love" to choose to abide,
In it forever.

LOVE REDEFINED
---------- (a Haiku) ----------
Rediscovering
The same heart with new purpose,
Redefining "love."

METASEX
---------- (a Haiku) ----------
What is beyond sex??
Complicated confusion,
Emotions and flesh.

TERM BREAKDOWN
---------- (a Haiku) ----------
Let's consider this...
The term "I'll make love to you"
Can we break that down??

LOVE'S INTENT

---------- (a Haiku) ----------

I truly believe,
Love is separate from sex,
Love speaks to intent.

The intent to please,
Unselfishly satisfy,
The heart of someone.

Maybe from hunger,
Or the burden of late bills,
Purposeful giving.

LOVE'S MEANING

---------- (a Haiku) ----------

Saying 'I love you'
Should mean "I am committed...
Through the good and bad"

"The sunshine and rain..."
"In times of plenty and lack..."
"(Know) I've got your back."

LIFE OF LOVE
---------- (a Haiku) ----------
If I walk in love...,
Live, breathe, sleep and die in "love,"
Does that mean I've loved??

THE GIFT OF LOVE
---------- (a Haiku) ----------
Did I waste my gift??
Simply potential untapped,
Like many of us.

LOVE'S PRIORITY
---------- (a Haiku) ----------
Love is to be shared,
Through a smile or charity,
(First) give to yourself.

LOVE'S TANK
---------- (a Haiku) ----------
Can one really give,
What they truly don't possess??
That's impossible.

LOVE'S CONFESSION
---------- (a Haiku) ----------
Well, I must admit,
Looking back over my life,
I never knew "love."

How could I really...?
When I didn't love myself...
Was I pretending??

I don't believe so...,
Although I do feel some shame,
I apologize.

For my flawed insight...,
Because what I felt for you,
Was much more than real.

REJECTED LOVE
---------- (a Haiku) ----------
Arbitrary love,
One-sided convenience,
A love unwelcomed.

LOVE'S PIMP
---------- (a Haiku story) ----------
With one exception,
I prostituted my love,
A woman - my pimp.

Desperate for love,
And without knowing its worth,
A true "bottom bitch".

Allured by sweet words,
Deceptive and promising,
Gullible I was.

Thirsty and naive,
Just like Anita Baker,
I loved "Just Because".

I recall a time,
I disappointed this pimp,
But soon faced regret.

Severe tongue lashings,
Abandonment then silence,
What she used to get.

No explanation,
The abused now abuser,
All because of fear.

An unresolved past,
Tainting the beauty of now,
Baggage held for years.

Allah rescued me,
Her intentions were not pure,
Simply running game.

When the well runs dry,
And love's a faint memory,
Life is not the same.

So I made the choice,
To just abandon that pimp,
I cannot stand pain.

A wrong is still wrong,
Just because I'm in prison,
That fact will not change.

Time is always proof,
Of the true nature of man,
Truth outlives a lie.

I forgave myself,
For choosing to be a whore,
My heart I denied.

With healing comes peace,
A brand new outlook on love,
Refreshing and free.

Pimps are not welcomed,
In my life forevermore,
I choose to love Me.

LOVE'S GOODBYE
---------- (a Haiku) ----------

So how does it feel,
To be abandoned by love,
And left all alone??

OFF-LIMITS LOVE
-------- (a Haiku confession) --------

A man weeps sometimes,
Tearless and untraceable,
The pain held within.

Emotional tears,
A hemorrhaged bleeding heart,
Scarred eternally.

Suspect - Anyone,
Uncertain and ungrateful,
Spoiling the whole bunch.

Trust? - impossible
Vulnerable? - unlikely
Please don't waste your time.

PART TWO

Lust

DEJA VU
---------- (a Haiku) ----------
Remember these lips?
The right amount of suction,
Brought tears to your eyes.

A GROWN WOMAN
---------- (a Haiku memory) ----------
I can remember,
A lady-friend once told me,
"Grown women swallow."

What?! Now you tell me,
All this time I have wasted?
Please make my toes curl.

You are so nasty,
I sure like that about you,
You really did it!!

Did you take my soul?
I feel a little lighter,
Truly life-changing.

POLE DANCER

---------- (a Haiku memory) ----------

I know this woman,
So doggone fine I wonder,
If she wears panties.

If she does wear them,
The fabric must be honored,
Just to touch her skin.

15

M. I. A.

---------- (a Haiku memory) ----------

Something frustrating;
My heart keeps yearning for you;
O distant lover.

The sweetest nectar,
Faint traces still slick my tongue,
Flowing climaxes.

Teardrop-stained pillows,
Whispers of painful pleasure,
Too good to be true.

Remember my curve?
The way I made you squeeze me,
With muscles untrained?

Until you submit,
I will always be to you,
One **Missed In Action**.

PANAMA

---------- (a Haiku memory) ----------

Sacred memory,
Encounter of raw passion,
Unfinished business.

How could you withhold,
The unparalleled pleasure,
Of hearing your voice??

Deeply personal,
This connection we both share,
Lasting beyond time.

JADED BY JODY
---------- (a Haiku) ----------
Whispered in your ear,
Repeated in submission,
Desired within.

Always remembered,
Within the pores of your skin,
Lasting impression.

Your daydream subject,
A feeling like yesterday,
So much more than real.

Mumbled in your sleep,
Causing your husband to ask,
'What did you just say?!"

'Whose name did you call?'
SALAHUDDIN is the name,
I apologize.

RECIPROCATION
---------- (a Haiku) ----------
Since you took my soul,
Let me return the favor,
And this won't take long.

I miss those grey eyes,
The bounce and sway of your hips,
And rubbing wet lips.

My desire - tease you,
Soaked panties with throbbing clit,
Wait - I'll be right back

One prophylactic,
Much better safe than sorry,
Touch yourself for me.

Do what you are told,
And just submit to my lust,
This is just the head.

Relax, this won't hurt,
How bout you take a deep breath,
Just inhale slowly.

There you go baby,
Just a little more to go,
I want you to squeeze.

You must concentrate,
Squeeze it tight, and then release,
Now do it again.

You ready to cum?
Turn this way just a little,
You sure you're ready?

What is the problem?
Why are you shaking like that?
You think you love me?

LOL- girl stop!
It's both a gift and a curse,
Making you explode.

You say you want more?
You'd better pick up the phone,
And order pizza.

PART THREE

Confusion

THE COUNTY JAIL
---------- (a Haiku memory) ----------

What is due process?
Theory never upheld,
Without some money.

A courtroom drama,
Manipulators of law,
For their agenda.

District Attorney,
The chosen voice of the state,
Inventor of lies.

Crooked county judge,
Too cavalier doing wrong,
For immunity.

Guilty innocence,
Admit guilt, and you can go,
The cost of freedom.

Too painful to read?
Imagine living this truth,
Utter confusion.

SNAPSHOT
---------- (a Haiku) ----------
The power of words,
More vivid than a picture,
A snapshot of time.

DOING TIME
---------- (a Haiku) ----------
A Monday morning,
Back to the same old routine,
Expecting breakthrough.

HOLDING ON
---------- (a Haiku) ----------
My heart beats with hope,
While tears carry my burdens,
Hoping change will come.

DARK TIMES
---------- (a Haiku) ----------
Dark times really help,
Me to focus on the light,
And all that it means.

CROSSROAD
---------- (a Haiku observation) ----------
Location - unknown,
Destiny undetermined,
Which way do I go??

You been here before??
Lonely nights and boring days,
Hoping for better.

But what is "better"??
I'm grateful for what I have
Just hoping for change.

Change in company,
Change in living location,
A permanent change.

THE RELIEF OF CHANGE
---------- (a Haiku) ----------
No more suffering,
The end of deliberate,
Abuse of power.

THE REWARD OF CHANGE
---------- (a Haiku) ----------

Abundant ice cream,
Dinner when I want to eat,
And no more "lockdown!"

ANOTHER ONE
---------- (a Haiku) ----------

That day will soon come,
When this will all be over,
Another 'crossroad'.

EMPTY
---------- (a Haiku observation) ----------

Feeling of weakness,
Exhausted from the release,
Tired of crying.

IT IS WHAT IT IS
---------- (a Haiku) ----------

You can do nothing,
My problems are internal,
And this too shall pass.

AL-ISLAM
---------- (a Haiku observation) ----------
Islam is a way,
To find true peace in your heart,
Along the straight path..

AS-SALAAM
---------- (a Haiku memory) ----------
Oh how true it is,
Allah is the "Source of Peace,"
For everyone.

TAKBEER
---------- (a Haiku observation) ----------
"Allah-who ak-bar"
And do you know what that means??
"Allah is most great"

WUDU'
---------- (a Haiku) ----------
My heart's intention,
Simple purification
Washing sins away.

SALAH
---------- (a Haiku) ----------
My life - I press 'pause,'
To ask Allah for guidance,
On this life journey.

ZAKAT
---------- (a Haiku) ----------
A fraction of wealth,
Remembering those without,
Just to please Allah.

TAWAKKUL
---------- (a Haiku) ----------
"Trusting" is so hard,
When you believe (you) know best,
Wait until you're crushed.

Then you will submit,
To all that has been decreed,
That's all that it took.

HYPOCRITES
---------- (a Haiku observation) ----------

"I'm Muslim" they claim,
Pretenders wanting control,
In prison that is...

The men of deceit,
Worshipers of their desires
How can you lead me??

Who is leading you??
And just where are you going??
Paradise or Hell??

MY TURN
---------- (a Haiku memory) ----------

I remember you,
You stabbed me in the heart twice,
The table has turned.

This may hurt a bit,
And this will last a lifetime,
The pain of regret.

BEYOND THESE WALLS
---------- (a Haiku reflection) ----------
Some "free-world" people,
Have no sense of loyalty,
You know who you are.

The great pretenders,
Ten toes down when you are up,
Nowhere to be found.

When this season ends,
Please don't act like you know me,
We were never friends.

Friendship is support,
Effort and consistency,
That something you lack.

Basic sign language,
A simple gesture will do,
Two middle fingers.

ABOUT THE AUTHOR

Autley I. Salahuddin is an American Muslim whose compelling journey and unique perspective profoundly shape his work. Born the eldest of two, he was nurtured and reared in an Islamic-influenced environment of education, hard work, discipline, and truth. His mother, a master of the craft of language, and his father, a seasoned counselor grounded in the practice of science, shaped his early life.

In his elemental years, his father inspired him to do "extra" to become extraordinary. Later, in his adolescence, his mother challenged him to be brave enough "to paint his own portrait on this canvas we call life," a philosophy that profoundly influenced the raw, unapologetic verses of his debut collection, *Haikus of Soul: Love, Lust & Confusion.*

Convinced he could accomplish anything, he launched his first business as a disc-jockey at the age of 16. This early venture was just the beginning of a diverse professional journey, including leveraging opportunities in Corporate America and within the Union after completing a rigorous apprenticeship. These experiences laid the groundwork for his eventual venture as the founder of OmniWorks International.

Guided by a destiny toward submission to Allah's Will, his journey has been defined by balancing life as an American Muslim. He grappled with retaining his integrity and faith amidst a country of ever-broadening "freedoms" and unlimited temptations, a struggle that uniquely shapes his perspective.

He is the founder and managing partner of OmniWorks International, a father to none, a brother to some, and a willing servant for all. Through his work and his words, he is an advocate for mental health awareness and aims to illuminate pathways for understanding and connection.

NOTES

NOTES

DID YOU ENJOY THIS BOOK?

We at OmniWorks International would love to know if

Haikus of Soul: Love, Lust & Confusion

resonated with your heart in any way.

Send your letters or cards to:

OmniWorks International
2950 Northwest 99 Street
Miami, FL 33147

www.ingramcontent.com/pod-product-compliance
Lightning Source LLC
Chambersburg PA
CBHW070651130626
46555CB00006B/2818